CORAL REEFS
AND
THEIR ANIMALS FRIENDS

SPEEDY
PUBLISHING

Speedy Publishing LLC
40 E. Main St. #1156
Newark, DE 19711
www.speedypublishing.com

The Great Barrier Reef
is the largest coral reef
system in the world.

Coral reefs are made up of live organisms. These organisms are tiny little animals called polyps. Coral reefs are generally found in clear, tropical oceans.

The coral reef is one of the major marine biomes. Around 25% of the known marine species live in coral reefs.

Coral reef ecosystems help remove and recycle carbon dioxide. They also protect land from harsh weather by absorbing the impact from strong waves and storms.

Corals grow in different shapes depending on their species. Coral reefs take a very long time to grow. They grow at a rate up to 2 cm per year.

Sea anemones look like flowers but are actually animals. They are related to both jellyfish and coral.

There are more than 1,000 sea anemone species found throughout the ocean. Anemones tend to stay in the same spot until a predator attacks them.

Clownfish are
bright orange fish
with three vertical
white stripes down their
sides. Clownfish have a
symbiotic relationship
with sea anemone.

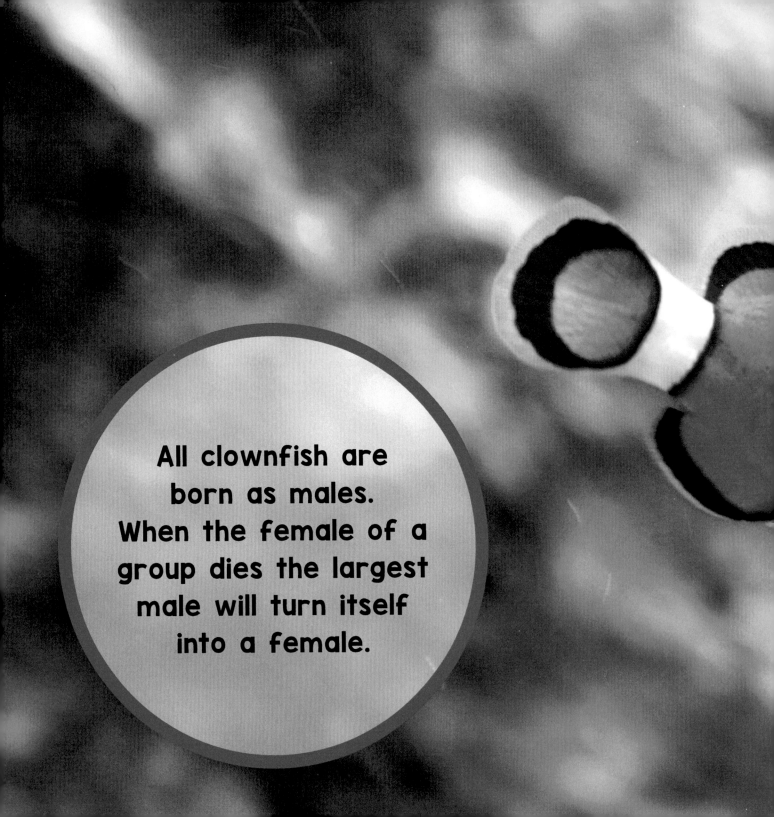

All clownfish are
born as males.
When the female of a
group dies the largest
male will turn itself
into a female.

Sea urchins have globe-like shape of the body that is covered with large number of long spines. Sea Urchins have over 200 species.

Sea Urchins typically range in size from 6 to 12 cm. Their spines are about 1 to 3 cm in length.

A seahorse is a
unique fish that mainly
lives in coastal areas
of oceans and seas.
There are over 50
seahorse species.

Seahorses vary in size from 0.6 to 14 inches in length. Seahorses are the slowest swimmers in the ocean.

Turtles are reptiles. They have a hard shell that protects them like a shield, this upper shell is called a carapace and the lower shell is called a plastron.

Sea turtles can be found throughout the world and in every ocean except for the Arctic Ocean.